ONE
Inner Child
SPEAKS

ELIZABETH GRIEST

Inks and Bindings
888-290-5218
www.inksandbindings.com
orders@inksandbindings.com

Contents

Introductory Letter

Hi Readers,

I'm an inner child, I hold my Adult Self's deepest feelings/ needs/ wants/ Beliefs about myself/ others/ Life/ God. I also hold the Blue Print of Adult Self's / my Sacred Life Purpose.

My Adult Self helped write this journal.

If you want, Readers, you can write your own Inner Child and/or Big Self works on the lined spaces.

God Bless us all.

----Little Kitten----

I

Sometimes I feel like nobody loves or understands me.

Then my Adult or Big Self reassures me she loves/understands me; and, so does God.

_____

_____

_____

_____

_____

_____

_____

_____

_____

_____

_____

_____

_____

_____

_____

_____

_____

_____

_____

II

I'm Little Kitten. My Adult Self is Big Kitten.

We believe God is Mother/ Father.

We believe God is Our Sacred Parents of All.

_____

_____

_____

_____

_____

_____

_____

_____

_____

_____

_____

_____

_____

_____

_____

_____

_____

_____

_____

_____

III

Big kitten sometimes overwhelms me by not protecting me enough.

By not defending me enough, by squelching me when I want to tell or show her something.

BK (short for Big Kitten) lets me down when she tries to overplease other people. But then, I can do that, too because I'm afraid they'll be angry at me, even abandon me, if I don't do exactly what they want me to.

_____

_____

_____

_____

_____

_____

_____

_____

_____

_____

_____

_____

_____

IV

I show BK what I feel/ want/ need at times via our body.

That can mean pains or exhaustion or dizziness when I feel someone or something is bad for me.

When someone or something is good for me, I can show a soothing warmth in our Solar Plexus, or restfulness, or a sense of balance.

_____

_____

_____

_____

_____

_____

_____

_____

_____

_____

_____

_____

_____

_____

_____

_____

V

My bodily health has to come first.

Our Sacred Parents of All can Guide/ Guard BK and me. If we let Them.

_____

_____

_____

_____

_____

_____

_____

_____

_____

_____

_____

_____

_____

_____

_____

_____

_____

_____

VI

I don't want to be a slave to others' opinions – especially about me.

I don't want to be a slave seeking others' approval.

_____

_____

_____

_____

_____

_____

_____

_____

_____

_____

_____

_____

_____

_____

_____

_____

_____

_____

_____

_____

VII

I want to Worship God in the Way that makes Sacred Sense to BK and me.

_____

_____

_____

_____

_____

_____

_____

_____

_____

_____

_____

_____

_____

_____

_____

_____

_____

_____

_____

_____

_____

VIII

I Want/Need the Right Man for me/ BK.

The man who really sees me/ values me/ BK.

And, who is assertive but not aggressive.

_____

_____

_____

_____

_____

_____

_____

_____

_____

_____

_____

_____

_____

_____

_____

_____

_____

_____

IX

To make things shorter/easier, I just say me when I mean BK and me.

She and I are inseparable.

X

Sometimes it's not easy being an Inner Child.

Sometimes I'm not listened to enough. Sometimes I'm not loved enough.

Sometimes I feel so alone/ so helpless/ so abandoned

_____

_____

_____

_____

_____

_____

_____

_____

_____

_____

_____

_____

_____

_____

_____

_____

_____

_____

XI

❖

BK and Mama/ Papa God remind me to turn to them when I'm feeling all scared and alone. And all confused.

_____

_____

_____

_____

_____

_____

_____

_____

_____

_____

_____

_____

_____

_____

_____

_____

_____

_____

_____

XII

Sometimes people forget the Inner Child is Sacred.

But, the Inner Child knows; for, somewhere deep down in everyone's Heart the Inner Child knows.

No matter how badly the Child Self may have been treated, the Heart-Knowing is alive.

_____

_____

_____

_____

_____

_____

_____

_____

_____

_____

_____

_____

_____

_____

_____

_____

_____

XIII

Somewhere in everyone's Mind there's a Knowing of the Inner Child being Sacred.

It's so, even if people are unaware sometimes that it's so.

_____

_____

_____

_____

_____

_____

_____

_____

_____

_____

_____

_____

_____

_____

_____

_____

_____

_____

_____

XIV

Bad treatment from others and myself—
especially from myself—can make me feel/ think
I'm not Sacred.

But, then I need to turn to Mama/ Papa God of
All to remind BK and me I am Sacred.

_____

_____

_____

_____

_____

_____

_____

_____

_____

_____

_____

_____

_____

_____

_____

_____

XV

Good treatment from others and myself—
particularly myself—can help me feel/ think I
am Sacred.

Still, BK and I need to keep reminding ourselves
the most important Knowing comes from
Mama/Papa God. They know I am Sacred.

_____

_____

_____

_____

_____

_____

_____

_____

_____

_____

_____

_____

_____

_____

_____

_____

_____

XVI

—◆·❈·❈·◆—

BK and I pray for Mama/ Papa God to Deep Heal us.

XVII

BK and I pray for Mama/ Papa God to help BK and me love each other.

XVIII

BK and I want the right man for us.

The Inner Boy of the right man for BK and me will be happy with me.

The Inner Boy will like my High- Sensitivity, Empathy, Loyalty.

He will not criticize or ridicule me.

He will do Nice things for me like walking with me—not ahead of me—and opening doors for me. Yes, besides honestly listening to me and giving me gifts.

_____

_____

_____

_____

_____

_____

_____

_____

_____

_____

_____

_____

XIX

I want to love myself. I want to clearly see my strengths. I want to clearly see my talents.

I want to value my strengths and talents.

I want to use my strengths and talents to benefit myself and others.

I want/ need You, Sacred Parents of All to help me see/ value/ use my strengths/ talents.

_____

_____

_____

_____

_____

_____

_____

_____

_____

_____

_____

_____

_____

_____

XX

BK/ I ask Sacred Parents of All to send us Sacred Synchronicities.

XXI

BK/I ask Divine Parents of All to send us Sacred Helpers—Heavenly ones and human ones.

_____

_____

_____

_____

_____

_____

_____

_____

_____

_____

_____

_____

_____

_____

_____

_____

_____

_____

XXII

BK/ I ask Sacred Parents of All to help BK/ me be a human helper to people and animals who Divine Parents of All want us to be.

XXIII

Sacred Parents of All, remind me/ BK over and over and over our soul frequency (energy)/ prayers/ writing are needed on Earth, or else BK/ I wouldn't be here.

_____

_____

_____

_____

_____

_____

_____

_____

_____

_____

_____

_____

_____

_____

_____

_____

_____

_____

_____

XXIV

Sacred Parents of All, use BK's/ my contemplations, conversations with other people, circumstances, etc. to remind us we're necessary on Earth.

Reminders happen daily.

_____

_____

_____

_____

_____

_____

_____

_____

_____

_____

_____

_____

_____

_____

_____

_____

_____

_____

_____

_____

XXV

From my earliest years on, I've been interested in how men can feel, think, speak, act differently from how women can.

XXVI

BK/ I want Sacred Companionship.

Please, Sacred Parents of All, Give us Sacred Companions.

_____

_____

_____

_____

_____

_____

_____

_____

_____

_____

_____

_____

_____

_____

_____

_____

_____

_____

_____

_____

XXVII

Please, Sacred Parents of All, help BK/ me be Sacred Companions to the Sacred Companions you give us.

XXVIII

Please, Divine Parents of All, Give me Divine Companions of this world, plus, Divine Companions of the Next World.

Thank You, Divine Parents of All.

XXIX

Please, Sacred Parents of All, help BK/me be a
Sacred Companion to Your Sacred Companions
of this world and Next World.

_____

_____

_____

_____

_____

_____

_____

_____

_____

_____

_____

_____

_____

_____

_____

_____

_____

_____

XXX

Please, Divine Parents of All, even if BK/ I don't always say Please and Thank You to You, BK/I mean it.

_____

_____

_____

_____

_____

_____

_____

_____

_____

_____

_____

_____

_____

_____

_____

_____

_____

_____

_____

_____

_____

XXXI

Please, Sacred Parents of All, Give BK/me companions who help us feel safe/ secure. This means male and female companions.

Thank You, Divine Parents of All.

_____

_____

_____

_____

_____

_____

_____

_____

_____

_____

_____

_____

_____

_____

_____

_____

_____

_____

_____

_____

XXXII

Please, Sacred Parents of All, help BK/ me be a companion who helps others feel safe/secure.

All through You, Divine Parents of All.

_____

_____
_____
_____
_____
_____
_____
_____
_____
_____
_____
_____
_____
_____
_____
_____
_____
_____
_____
_____

XXXIII

Sacred Parents, BK/ I would really like to have a small dog companion.

We like 'pushed in' face type such as a Pekingese, or Japanese Chin, or Tibetan Spaniel or Havanese. Could be a Pug.

Please, Sacred Parents of All, give us the doggie meant for BK/ me.

_____

_____

_____

_____

_____

_____

_____

_____

_____

_____

_____

_____

_____

_____

XXXIV

Divine Parents, BK/ I often fear other peoples' disapproval.

It really HURTS when people verbally attack BK's/ my Beliefs and Writing.

You Understand, Divine Parents of All.

_____

_____

_____

_____

_____

_____

_____

_____

_____

_____

_____

_____

_____

_____

_____

_____

_____

_____

XXXV

Sacred Parents of All, help BK/ me see verbal attackers are afraid. Scared by my Beliefs and Writing because they don't match attackers' Beliefs.

_____

_____

_____

_____

_____

_____

_____

_____

_____

_____

_____

_____

_____

_____

_____

_____

_____

_____

_____

_____

XXXVI

Divine Parents of All, help BK/ me be understanding toward our verbal attackers.

But! Help BK/ me be Kitten Courageous who courteously/ clearly/ completely stands by our Beliefs/ Writing.

Thank You, Sacred Parents of All, who loves me/ everyone SO MUCH.

_____

_____

_____

_____

_____

_____

_____

_____

_____

_____

_____

_____

_____

_____

_____

XXXVII

Sacred Parents of All, help me be patient when people keep BK/ me waiting.

But! Please don't let them do it too often.

_____

_____

_____

_____

_____

_____

_____

_____

_____

_____

_____

_____

_____

_____

_____

_____

_____

_____

_____

_____

_____

_____

XXXVIII

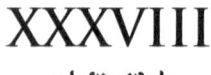

Divine Parents of All, please help me gently inform those who keep BK/ me unnecessarily waiting that BK's/ my time and energy are as valuable as anyone's.

_____

_____

_____

_____

_____

_____

_____

_____

_____

_____

_____

_____

_____

_____

_____

_____

_____

_____

_____

_____

_____

_____

XXXIX

Sometimes, Divine Parents, BK/ I just want to be hermits.

Especially I want to because I can be so easily hurt.

You Understand BK/ me.

_____
_____
_____
_____
_____
_____
_____
_____
_____
_____
_____
_____
_____
_____
_____
_____
_____

XL

Divine Parents, You help BK/ me—especially me—Understand You Give us our High Sensitivity so we can help others and ourselves.

XLI

Divine Parents of All, You show BK/ me You don't want us to be a hermit, a recluse.

You bring people into BK's/ my life for us to interact with.

But, please bring only Kind/ Courteous Individuals.

_____

_____

_____

_____

_____

_____

_____

_____

_____

_____

_____

_____

_____

_____

_____

_____

XLII

Sacred Parents of All, if You must bring less than Kind/ Courteous people to me, help me be Courteous—and, if necessary Kind.

Help BK/ me turn to You for Comfort/ Reassurance of Your Love.

_____
_____
_____
_____
_____
_____
_____
_____
_____
_____
_____
_____
_____
_____
_____
_____
_____
_____

XLIII

Sacred Parents of All, Help BK/ me be strong and sensitive.

_____

_____

_____

_____

_____

_____

_____

_____

_____

_____

_____

_____

_____

_____

_____

_____

_____

_____

_____

_____

_____

_____

XLIV

Divine Parents of All, Help BK/ me be strong in <u>Your</u> Ways in dealing with life and people.

_____

_____

_____

_____

_____

_____

_____

_____

_____

_____

_____

_____

_____

_____

_____

_____

_____

_____

_____

_____

XLV

Help BK/ me, Divine Parents of All, be sensitive
in <u>Your</u> Ways in dealing with life and people.

_____

_____

_____

_____

_____

_____

_____

_____

_____

_____

_____

_____

_____

_____

_____

_____

_____

_____

_____

_____

XLVI

Often Help Remind BK/ me, Sacred Parents of All, to often Thank You for Your Gift of Writing. Because Writing is an important part of my Sacred Life Purpose.

_____

_____

_____

_____

_____

_____

_____

_____

_____

_____

_____

_____

_____

_____

_____

_____

_____

_____

_____

_____

XLVII

Often Help Remind BK/ me, Divine Parents of All, to often Thank You for your Gift of High Sensitivity.

XLVIII

---·✦·❖·❖·✦·---

Often Help Remind BK/ me, Divine Parents of All,
to often Thank You for Your Gift of Discernment.

XLIX

❖⸱⸱❖⸱⸱❖❖⸱⸱❖⸱⸱❖

Often Help Remind BK/ me, Sacred Parents of All,
Your Gift of Writing is to aid BK/ me and others.

_____

_____

_____

_____

_____

_____

_____

_____

_____

_____

_____

_____

_____

_____

_____

_____

_____

_____

_____

_____

_____

_____

L

Often Help Remind BK/ me, Divine Parents of All, Your Gift of High Sensitivity is to help BK/ me as well as others.

_____

_____

_____

_____

_____

_____

_____

_____

_____

_____

_____

_____

_____

_____

_____

_____

_____

_____

_____

_____

LI

---✦··❊❊❊❊❊❊❊❊··✦---

Often Help BK/ me remember, Sacred Parents of
All, Your Gift of Discernment is to benefit BK/
me and others.

LII

Sacred Parents of All, BK/ I Believe You Desire
All Your Children to live as Spiritual Aristocrats—
Honest/ Fair/ Courteous to themselves and everyone.

_____

_____

_____

_____

_____

_____

_____

_____

_____

_____

_____

_____

_____

_____

_____

_____

_____

_____

_____

_____

_____

LIII

BK/ I know, Divine Parents of All, You Desire BK/ me, all Your Children to often go beyond Courtesy to Kindness.

For that is Part of your Code of Spiritual Aristocracy.

_____

_____

_____

_____

_____

_____

_____

_____

_____

_____

_____

_____

_____

_____

_____

_____

_____

_____

_____

_____

LIV

Sacred Parents of All, BK/ I know You Desire BK/ me to be Kind to ourselves.

Because that is a Portion of Your Way of Spiritual Aristocracy.

LV

Divine Parents of All, BK/ I know You Desire BK/ me to be Kind to others—people and animals.

For, that is Part of Your Code of Spiritual Aristocracy.

_____
_____
_____
_____
_____
_____
_____
_____
_____
_____
_____
_____
_____
_____
_____
_____
_____
_____
_____
_____
_____